Copyright © 2013 Katie Lei

All rights reserved. This book or any portion thereof may not be reproduced or used in any manner whatsoever without the express written permission of the author/artist except for the use of brief quotations in a book review.

ISBN: 978-1-304-55847-3

Doodlesdoes.wordpress.com

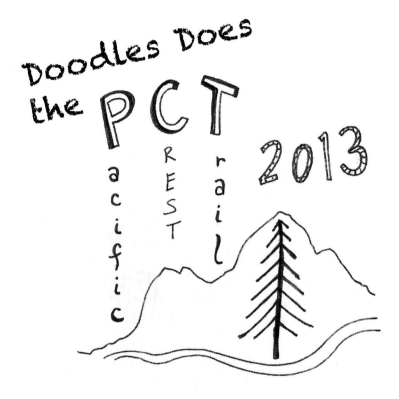

I would like to dedicate this book to my amazing friend, Claire, whithout whom I would have neither started the trail nor kept hiking nearly as far as I did. Thank you for being you!

BEFORE

My friend Claire and I have known each other since kindergarten and have been backpacking together since high school. We first heard about the Pacific Crest National Scenic Trail sometime back in middle school. This 2,668-mile hiker and equestrian trail starts at the Mexican Border outside of Campo, CA and ends in Manning Park, Canada after traversing California, Oregon, and Washington states. From the day we learned that such a trail existed, it became one of those things that we would "definitely do at some point," right alongside becoming a professional athlete or an astronaut. However, in late 2011, with less than a year left of college, we realized that this particular dream could actually be possible. So, sitting in Baker & Spice after a walk on a drizzly Portland fall day, we pulled out a napkin and agreed to plan our next two years around hiking the PCT...

> We, Claire and Katie, do hereby solemnly swear to make and uphold our epic plans to hike the Pacific Crest Trail together beginning in the Spring of the year 2013. Should either person fail to uphold this contract (for any reason other than death, serious health concerns, or abduction by aliens), her extreme failure will always be held against her, and she will be obligated to find ALL future coffee dates.
>
> This we do swear by all things baked and delicious, or relating to mountains,
>
> Katie Claire

So... in early 2013, we finalized our itinerary for the hike, bought two big shopping carts full of trail food, packed our resupply boxes for the California section of the trail and lined them up in my parents' basement with instructions for where and when to send them to us along the way. In late February, we packed up Moose (my car) with all the essentials for the next seven months, which we had decided to begin with a few shorter adventures. First we headed down to Flagstaff, Arizona, where we met up with friends for a 21-day rafting trip down the Colorado River in the Grand Canyon, during which I worked on my white-water kayaking and tested out the idea of keeping a trail journal in the form of drawings.

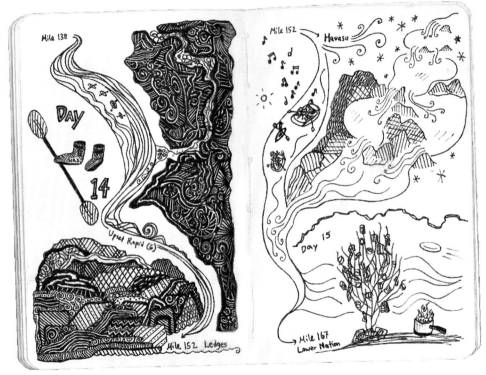

From there, we made our way over to Nevada, where we spent three weeks car camping and rock climbing at Red Rock Canyon National Conservation Area outside of Las Vegas. In late April, we finally made it down to the U.S.-Mexico border to begin our hike.

WAITING

We've pushed away from shore, and there's no more time for turning back.

Rounding a bend, I hear the churning water screaming and rumbling in the distance.

We've poured over the maps and discussed the line to take and the obstacles to avoid.

We've read the first-hand accounts and stories of those who've passed this way before us.

We know the difficulty rating and the dangers. The one-in-three success rate does nothing to calm my nerves as we float ever closer to the mounting thunder.

This rapid has a name - it is called the Pacific Crest Trail, and it is not the first or only rapid on this river.

Before this we had the Liberal Arts Rapids, Seasonal Employment Falls, Coming Home Riffles...

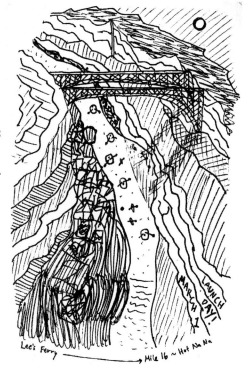

We only just made it through Lava Falls, and after this next drop we'll hit the even bigger stuff – Readjusting Rapid, Finding a Real Job Rapid, and miles and miles of turbulent water in the Now You're Supposed to Be an Adult section of the river.

But I can't think about all of that right now.

All I can see is the horizon line of the PCT as it gets closer and closer to my little boat, the fireworks of white foam shooting up from behind the steep drop.

We know the line, and we've practiced our rolls; we've broken in our shoes and packed our resupply boxes.

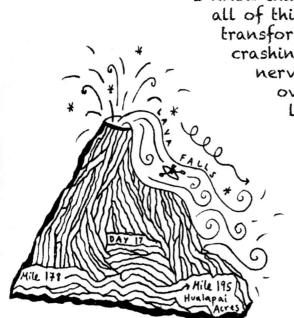

I know that once I hit that first big wave all of this anticipation and planning will transform into raw reactions to the crashing walls of icy water, and that nervous feeling in my stomach will be overshadowed by a rush of adrenaline that will help me through.

I line up on the boil line and set up to paddle hard left after the ledge hole.

We'll deal with the later rapids when they come, but for now all we need to do is stay in our boats and just start hiking.

2,350 Miles
147 Days
3 Pairs of Brooks Cascadias
3 Moleskine Notebooks
3 Fine Point Black Rollerball Pens
2 Trekking Poles
1 Osprey Backpack
1 Long Story to Share...

On our way. 2 days, 20 miles, we put our hands in Mexico then started our long walk North. Starting's the hardest part, we hear — it gets harder every day for the first 2 weeks, then easier every day right on through to Canada. Water's only a problem for the first 700 miles or so, according to a 2011 hiker, even when there's low snow in the Sierras. I do the math in my head... that's only 5 weeks of water stress, possibly the only thing worse than cheese stress. Nope, 5 weeks don't exist. There's just here to Warner Springs. There's just right now, sitting by the lake, listening to the chattering birds and distantly blasting music. There's just one day, one water source, one step at a time.

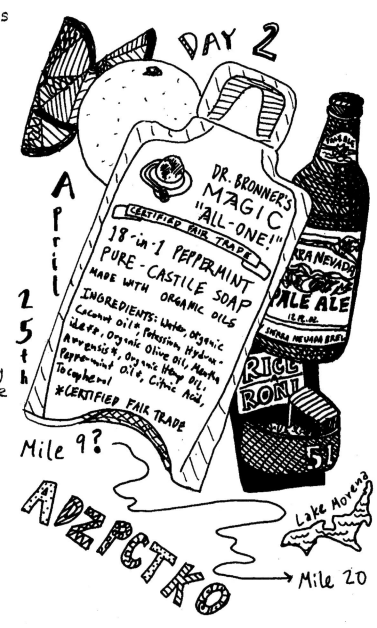

DAY 2
April 25th
Mile 9?
ADZPCTKO
Lake Morena
→ Mile 20

I woke up this morning and ran away to the lake. Walking fast, I held in my tears through the city of tents. I can't pinpoint exactly why I need to cry, but I do, so I give myself this time to sort it out.

Nearing a small collection of granite boulders, I immediately see gear placements and boulder problems. An apparently beautiful hand crack draws my attention and pulls me towards it. Upon closer examination, more of a fist crack. What am I doing here? I'm a climber, not a long-distance backpacker. The next 90 miles loom in my mind like the pool of fog over the lake in front of me, the thought of throbbing feet and aching shoulders blocking out all appreciation for the beauty of these hills and the fact that I do indeed want to be here.

I think back to a parallel feeling almost two months ago - I'm not a kayaker, I thought, cramming myself into a frighteningly tiny boat at Lee's Ferry, paralyzed by the unknown river ahead and the horrifying thought of getting stuck in the kayak. Then a month later, the same thing. Gazing up at the red rocks of the Calico Hills - What am I doing here? I'm not a climber, I'm a boater. After three weeks on the Colorado, the water had become my home, and that tiny kayak had become a part of me, an extension of my own legs floating me downstream. Now the thought of climbing rocks felt counterintuitive, foolish even, fighting against gravity only to end up back where you started, surrounded by nothing but harsh and unforgiving rock. But here I sit, now looking back fondly on those weeks of climbing, the slow and calm movements from one comfortable hold to another, the puzzle of placing the right piece of gear in the best feature in the rock, the bold decision to lead a sport route that may be too hard, the acrobatic nature of some climbs and that feeling of putting every ounce of strength into a single move. Those challenges now appeal to me, being familiar and therefore less intimidating than what lies ahead - hiking through hours and days of pain, not being sure how far to the next water source, being away for so long.

But I'm sensing a pattern. Maybe starting is always the hardest part. Maybe, 6 months from now, I'll look up at the welded tuff of Smith Rock and think - I'm not a climber, I'm a backpacker.

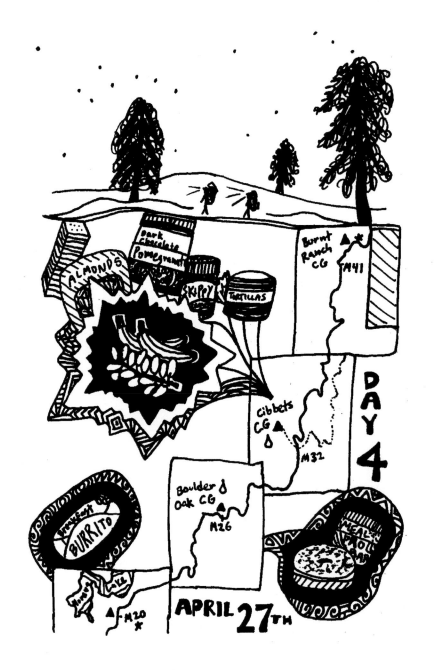

* TRAIL NAMES *

Out on the trail, most long-distance hikers acquire a "trail name," which is simply a nickname that they go by during their hike. Not far into the desert, I became "Doodles" and Claire became "Scones." Throughout this notebook, some doodles include rectangular boxes with words or names in them. These are the names or trail names of people we met or who were an important part of that day.

ODE TO A GIANT ASPARAGUS

Strolling up some switchbacks
I look to my left and see, towering above
all the other plants, a giant asparagus, green
and delicious-looking.

Dr. Seuss must have spent some time in the
desert, because his whimtastical worlds seem
normal next to what I've seen out here.
Apparently this is actually part of a yucca...
or an agave... I should have read up on my
desert botany before this trip.

But I don't care...
It looks like an asparagus, and I'd love to
chop it up and sauté it in some butter that
we don't have to eat with our tuna mac-and-
cheese tonight.

I'd also like a milkshake.

EARWIGS

MOTHS

CRAZY SUPER-SPEEDY SPIDER

ANTS

SCARY GIANT SPIDER

NORMAL TINY SPIDERS

Real-size* drawings of bugs sharing our campsite tonight (day 6).

*Except for giant spider... that was bigger in real life.

THE WAY OF THE WALKER

We wake up in the morning and we walk. We walk until it is too hot to walk. When it is too hot for walking we rest. We rest until the evening chases the afternoon away, and once it is no longer too hot we walk some more. We walk through valleys and hills and fatigue and foot pains. We walk with our backpacks and our daydreams. Words and pictures and invented stories drift through my mind while I watch the trail slide by under my feet. I imagine that Claire mostly dreams of cats, watching YouTube videos on a loop in her head as the trees pass by outside. Once in a while we speak, of our dreams or pains, of the trail or view, of anything or nothing at all. Sometimes we talk, but mostly we walk. We walk through trees and deserts until it is too dark to walk. When it is too dark for walking we rest. We rest until the sun chases the night away, and when it is no longer too dark we walk some more.

How do we judge ourselves out here? By the lightness of our packs? By the layers of dirt on our legs? By the mileages we hike?

Well, today my ankle/shin hurts and we're stopping for the day, maybe for tomorrow as well. So what does that make me? Useless is how I feel. Not as capable or competent as I had hoped to be. Fragile – from feeling great to barely being able to limp along with my pack in less than an hour.

We only had three more miles to go for water and shade, but what if it had been more? What if something like this happens in the middle of the Mojave? I feel exposed, suddenly unable to ignore how vulnerable we are out here.

I was thinking in terms of our schedule, of making miles, of staying ahead of the crowds. But that's not what this really about. Now I think it's just about being here. It's about taking care of each other. It may even be about learning to re-evaluate how we judge ourselves.

DAY 10
MAY 3RD

Mile 127 → Mile 137

Happy Mothers Day!

NORTH

Walking fast they follow their shadows North. Haven't you heard, this is a race, and they're all in it to win. Walking into the sun is like going backwards, the wrong way, like walking down a flight of stairs only to climb back up. Why would you pay attention in class when you could be counting down 'til 3 o'clock? Why would you ever slow down when you have the option to speed up? Rushing ever faster towards that glimmering trophy of success, completion, the end. Counting down the miles and the days, they forget. They forget that the trail does not know their time scale or their goals, that it is gracefully indifferent to their imagined concepts of progress and success. The trail is not a road to a destination, not a straight line pointing efficiently North. True to the landscapes it occupies, it leads them up and down, East and West and even South, around this and over that, through heat and cold and dry and moist. True to itself it leads them on, not forwards but back and forth, switch-backing deeper into the landscape and deeper into themselves. And it goes on and on, so that after days and weeks and hours and months they finally forget. They forget that they are waiting for the bell to ring at 3 and that life is about winning the race. They forget that walking South is moving away from the finish line. They forget that they have ever even imagined the idea of a finish line or a trophy. They forget everything but their footsteps, and themselves, and the trail that guides them along.

Mile 156

Hot Mess

Dr. Sole Town

Paradise Valley Café

Hwy 74

Turtle Silver

DAY 11
MAY 4TH

D.J. Feels Good

Mile 137

Some days I ask myself why I'm doing this. Most days I have a sufficient answer to justify whatever we're dealing with. But today, my hands frozen around my trekking poles and my rain jacket being pelted with rain and pine tree icicles, I couldn't remember any of my usual answers. I'm cold and wet and sad and singing country songs to myself, and I just want to go home. Walking along and trying to think of how to best write all of this down without sounding like I've just given up, we move off the trail to let a fellow hiker pass. As he goes by, as cold and wet as we are, he stops for a moment and hands us each a generous square of dark chocolate. And there it was, my answer for today handed to me out of a shiny gold wrapper in the darkest part of my day. Not the chocolate itself, but the gesture - a powerful reminder that, out here on the trail, we take care of each other.

I'm warmer now and still working on that question. Why am I out here? What am I willing to risk? How far out of my comfort zone am I willing to go? This has not been an easy trip so far, and I don't predict that it ever will be easy. There are comfortable moments, like right now at Ziggy and the Bear's, warm in my sleeping bag with my belly full of ice cream. The kindness and generosity of complete strangers repeatedly astonishes me. Like DNA with the sodas and beer and words of reassurance under the bridge today after the trudge across the windy sand field. Just when I'm ready to give up on the thought that this is where I want to be, some unexpected trail angel shows up to convince me otherwise. Thank you to all the trail angels we've met so far and to all the ones we'll meet later.

*Zero Day = A day with zero mileage. A rest day.

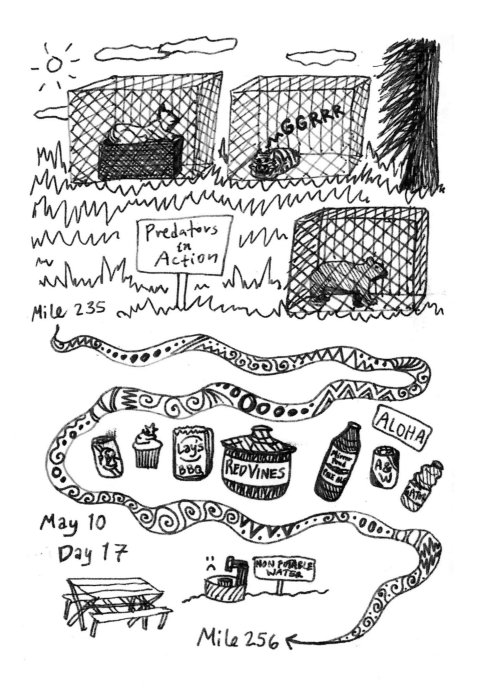

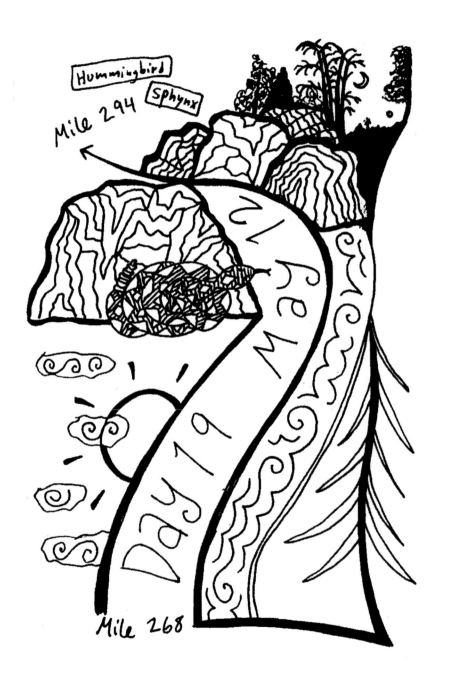

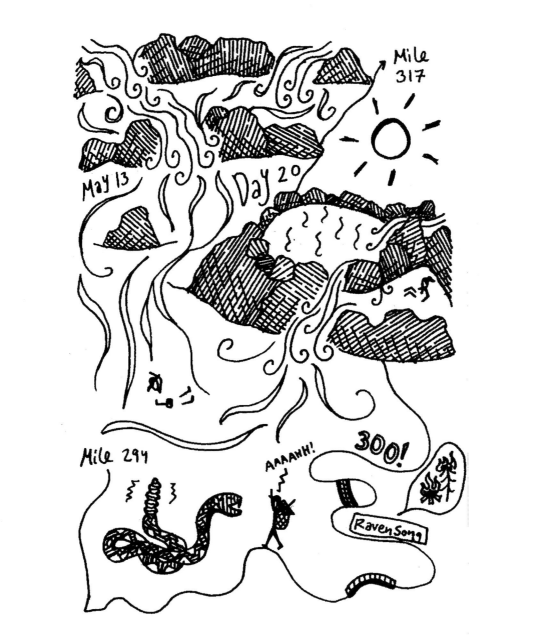

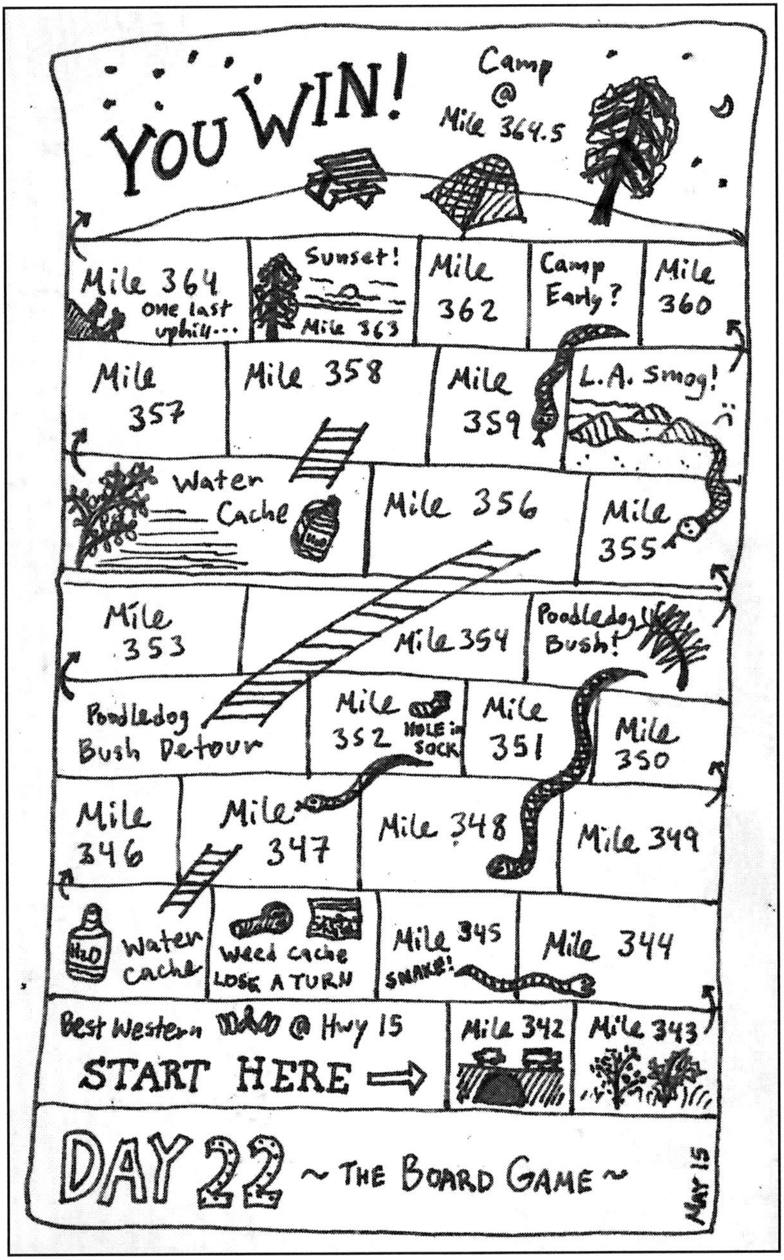

YOU WIN!

Camp @ Mile 364.5

Mile 364 one last uphill...	Sunset! Mile 363	Mile 362	Camp Early?	Mile 360
Mile 357	Mile 358	Mile 359	L.A. Smog!	
Water Cache		Mile 356	Mile 355	
Mile 353		Mile 354	Poodledog Bush!	
Poodledog Bush Detour	Mile 352 HOLE in SOCK	Mile 351	Mile 350	
Mile 346	Mile 347	Mile 348	Mile 349	
Water Cache	Weed Cache LOSE A TURN	Mile 345 SNAKE!	Mile 344	
Best Western @ Hwy 15 START HERE →		Mile 342	Mile 343	

DAY 22 ~ THE BOARD GAME ~

May 15

Mt. Baden-Powell!

Mile 394

← WRIGHTWOOD

Hwy 2

Mile 369.5

D A Y   2 4 ,   M A Y   1 7

BREAKFAST — quesadilla, o.j., ice cream bar

Frosty

2ND BREAKFAST! — bear claw

Rabbit Stick — cheezy bagel

BICYCLES

I'm flying. I'm literally flying right now. My arms out to the sides, the air rushing over my face and legs, the road and trees and fences rolling smoothly away, faster and faster...

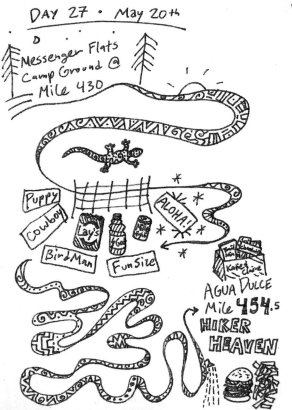

... Handlebars abandoned, I chart my course straight ahead simply by sitting up straight, I avoid the potholes with the slightest thought in the desired direction, I gain speed by letting gravity pull me down the gently inclined street. No effort from my legs, no weight on my back... ...

... ... I feel free and fast and fearless, and I want this hill to never end. Tomorrow I'll put my pack back on and move with slow and deliberate steps, one at a time, for hours and hours. Tomorrow I will walk, but right now I'm flying.

*Nero Day = A day with low mileage, usually less than 10 miles, and often in or out of a resupply.

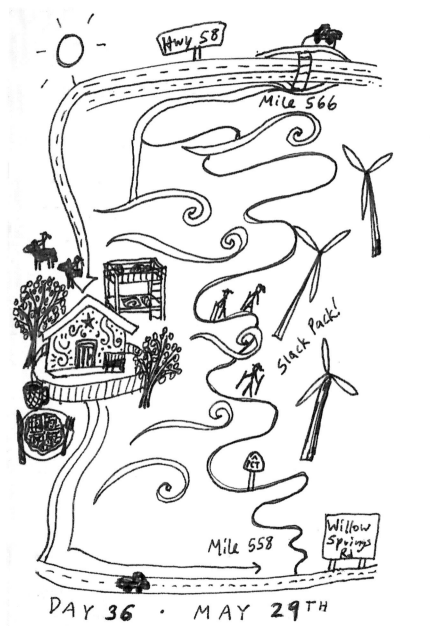

I come from the forest – from rivers and streams and hills and trees, from stinging nettles and blackberries and Western Red Cedars and Douglas Firs. I come from sword ferns and salmonberry bushes and clovers and chanterelles. The desert is vast and beautiful in its scope and simplicity, but its aged indifference to my existence reads as hostility. Perhaps because I do not know where to look, it offers neither nourishment nor shade, neither water nor shelter...

... It reminds me of my tininess and fragility, of those things that I need on the most basic level and of their true value. As I finally ascend back into the trees after three long months, the wind breathes through the tall grasses, and life rushes back into me. The birds and insects chirp their greetings, and the pine and oak trees compete to shelter me from the sun. These hills may be just as uninterested in my presence as the empty desert below, but it most certainly does not feel that way. Here I am safe and surrounded and at home. I came from the forest. Please don't send me back to the desert.

We woke up today and watched the sun rise over the Mojave. We turned our backs on the desert and walked up into the hills. Now we sit camped by a river, nothing but trees and mountains and stars in sight, the sound of running water lulling us to sleep. Sure, we'll have to worry about mosquitoes and bears from now on, but that's just because this is a place that can support life, and I'll take that over the desert any day.

Mile 674 → Mile 699

DAY 44

JUNE 6TH

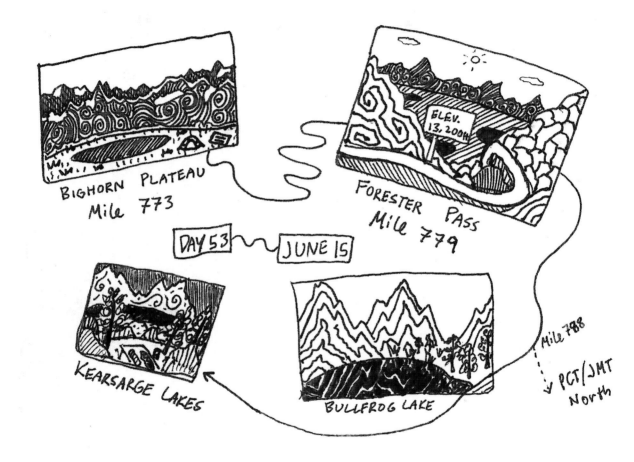

MOSQUITOES (ARE ASSHOLES)

They are everywhere. I try to watch my steps, but each swarm of hundreds and hundreds distracts me. Step to the right of the rock, turn to my left shoulder and slap at three of them, then to the right, the whole arm is covered and I brush them all off, look back down to avoid the root in the trail, now back to the left shoulder where I just felt one bite through my shirt below my head net. I can't take it any more...

... so I stop, swatting all around, throw off my pack, loosen the strap, reach in for my green rain jacket. The morning is already hot, and my impermeable pants and now top trap all of the sweat, soaking my base layers and nearly making me miss the desert, where at least there were no bugs, not like this at least. My ankles itch from where they poked through my socks, and my shoulders and wrists begin to complain as well. I smash one more into my rain pants, not because I believe it will bite through, but out of plain frustration and revenge for the discomfort all of its friends have already caused me. This is the one and only creature that I've ever taken pleasure in killing. No remorse whatsoever, just satisfaction. I clap another between my right fist and left sleeve, then tighten the synch on my net and anxiously await the evening, when I'll watch them through the mesh force-field of our tent and rest in safety until the morning.

TUOLUMNE MEADOWS

Store - Post Office - Grocery
Gifts - Camping - Ice

Day 66 - - June 28

Dance Party

Focus

Buff!

Mile 942

Mile 931

What John Muir has to say about zero days...

"Once I was let down into a deep well into which choke-damp had settled, and nearly lost my life. The deeper I was immersed into the invisible poison, the less capable I became of willing measures to escape from it. And in just this condition are those who toil or dawdle or dissipate in crowded towns, in the sinks of commerce or pleasure."

~ John Muir, September 1874, John of the Mountains, 191-92

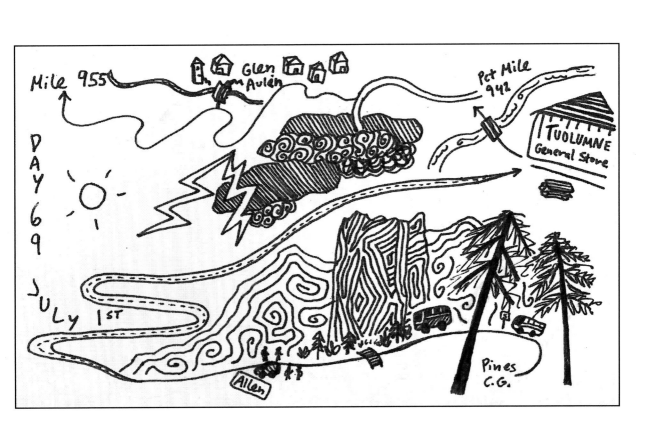

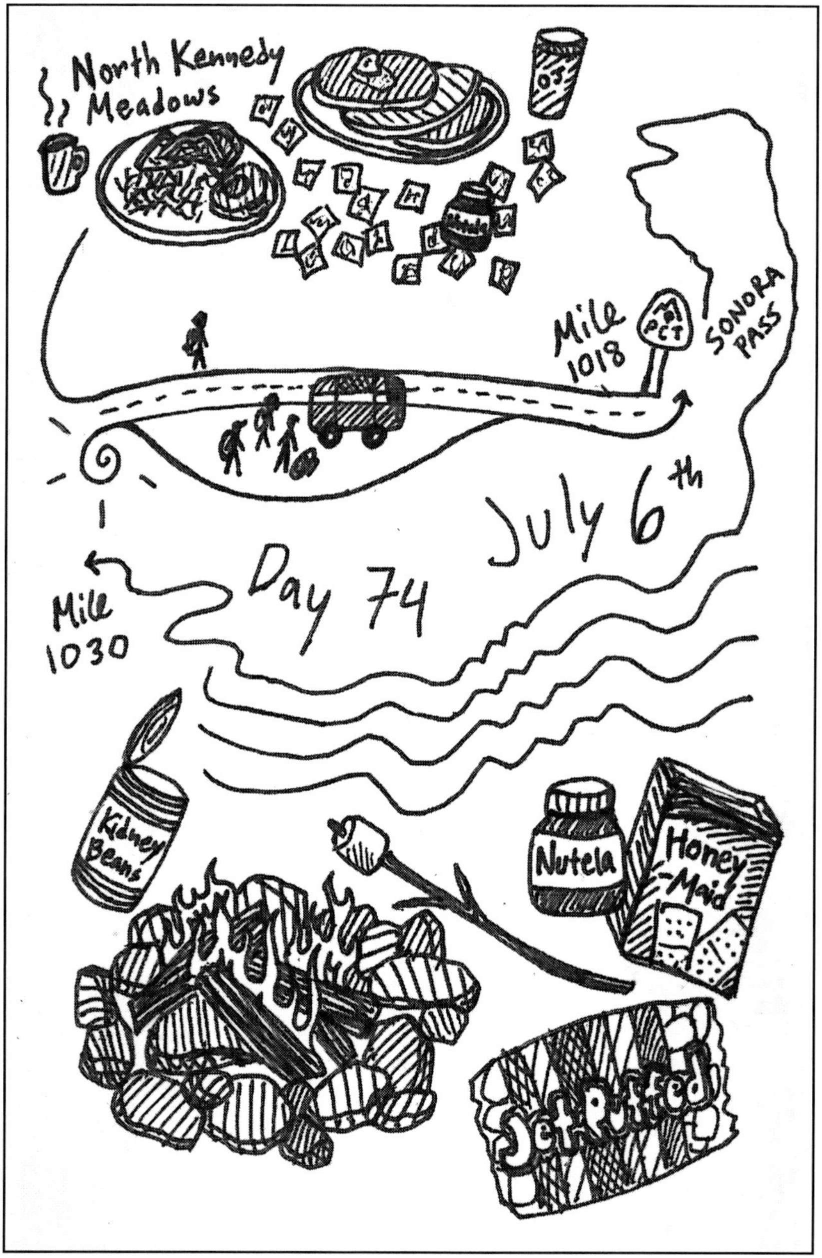

North Kennedy Meadows
OJ
Mile 1018
PCT
SONORA PASS
July 6th
Day 74
Mile 1030
Kidney Beans
Nutela
Honey-Maid
Jet-Puffed

THE ONES YOU KNOW WILL MAKE IT

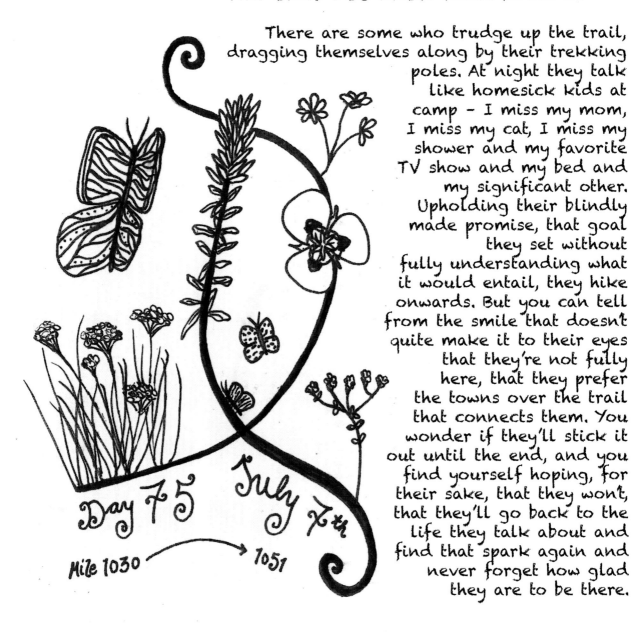

There are some who trudge up the trail, dragging themselves along by their trekking poles. At night they talk like homesick kids at camp – I miss my mom, I miss my cat, I miss my shower and my favorite TV show and my bed and my significant other. Upholding their blindly made promise, that goal they set without fully understanding what it would entail, they hike onwards. But you can tell from the smile that doesn't quite make it to their eyes that they're not fully here, that they prefer the towns over the trail that connects them. You wonder if they'll stick it out until the end, and you find yourself hoping, for their sake, that they won't, that they'll go back to the life they talk about and find that spark again and never forget how glad they are to be there.

Day 75   July 7th

Mile 1030 → 1051

Those are some of them.
Then there are the others, the ones with that gleam in their eyes. You see that spring in their step and you can tell that their feet don't hurt anymore, or that if they do they've learned to coexist with the pain, like the grizzled mountaineer who welcomes the cold like an old friend.
They walk on and drink in the clean mountain air, soaking in the trees and the flowers and the sun like a thirsty sponge finally allowed to expand in a clear alpine lake after years of compression between the concrete walls of city life and obligations. These ones do not talk much of home, nor of the future. They know that they are exactly where they need to be, and you can see that they want for nothing more than to remain in the here and the now.
These are the ones you know will make it, and you know they know it as well.

Those are the archetypes, the extremes. But you will meet few who fit into either box perfectly, especially since the box is only imagined and we all came out here to escape it. In reality we are more like pinball's, bouncing between extremes and dabbling in the whole spectrum of feelings towards the trail. We complain of aches and fatigue and then, suddenly struck by a new view, freeze and marvel wordlessly at that type of wild and open beauty that makes everything else seem distant and irrelevant. We hike on and choose our path anew each and every day, often balancing on that thin rail between GAME OVER and a straight shot North, into new trees and mountains and streams, into another day of unknown and adventure and life out in the open.

DAY 81 • MILE 1159 ⟶ MILE 1182 • JULY 13 •

Dear diary,
Today we discovered that Buff's new camera came with a disfunctional shutter button. The camera can take videos and do all sorts of things but cannot actually snap photos. Upon further investigation we discovered a variety of interesting settings, including one called CAT MODE, which automatically takes a picture when a cat's face is detected. Luckily, Claire happened to have some cat pictures on hand, and we were able to cut one out and use it to activate this feature by simply holding it up in front of whatever we wanted to capture in a photo. Thus, all pictures from today, whether they be of people or scenery, include our new friend, Adventure Cat.

MILE 1240
MILE 1262
DAY 85 JULY 17

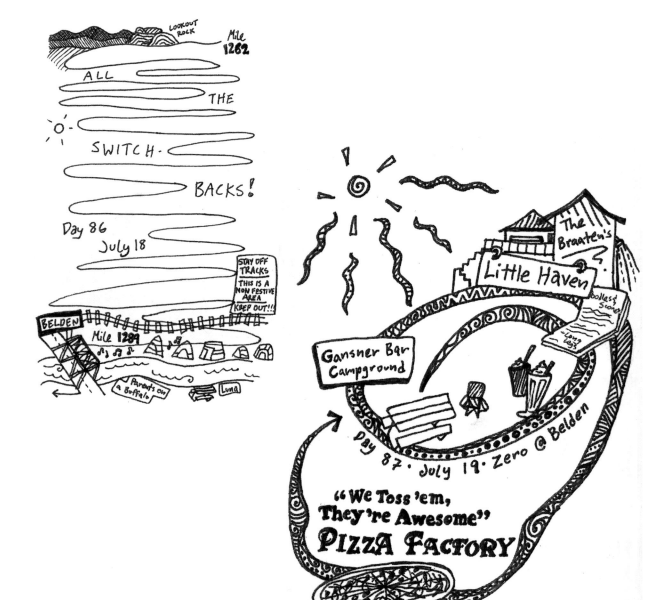

DAY 89 JULY 21ST

MILE 1294 → 1319

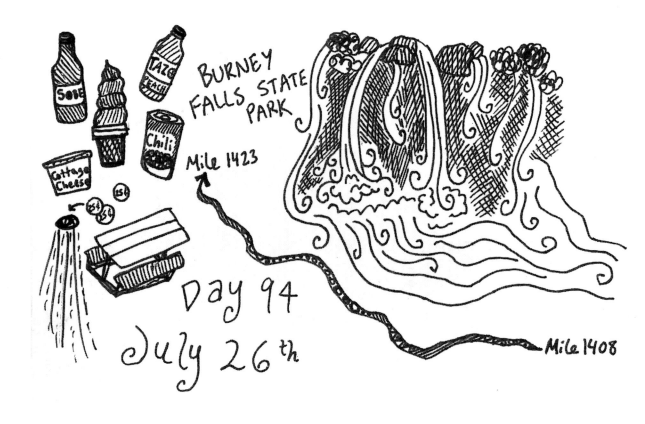

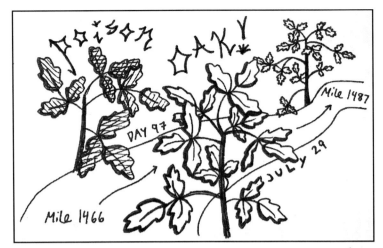

Apparently my athletically-induced asthma doesn't do well with forest fires. With all of the smoke in the air hiking up out of Castella, I found myself incapable of hiking uphill and breathing effectively at the same time. So Claire, Buff and I decided to reformulate the plan...

Buff | Scones | BEND → BLACK BUTTE ← SISTERS | Mommy

REI

Ray's

August Resupplies!

August 2, 2013 (Day 101)

THE NEW PLAN:

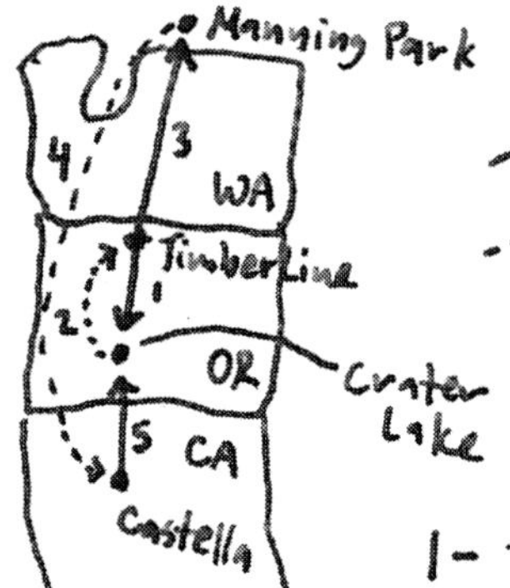

Manning Park
4 | 3 WA
Timberline
2
OR — Crater Lake
5 CA
Castella

→ = hike
--→ = shuttle/teleport

1 - Timberline Lodge to Crater Lake
3 - Timberline to Manning Park
5 - Castella to Crater Lake

* Avoid fires/smoke in CA & OR.
* Avoid October in northern WA

88% COCO

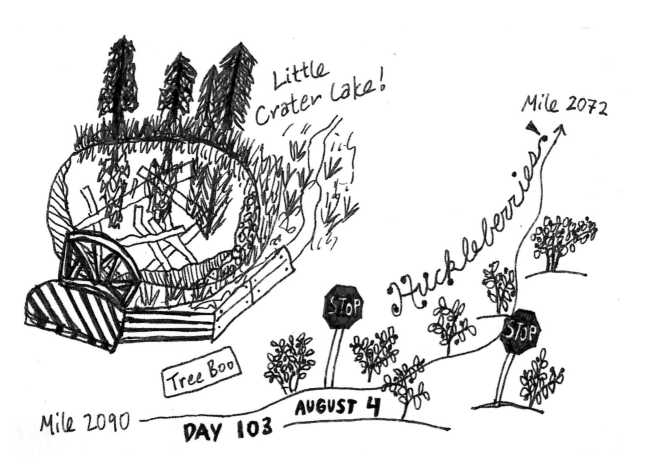

THIS FEELING

Don't forget this feeling.
When you are older and have a real job
and your own house and more than enough to get by,
don't forget how it felt to wonder if anyone would ever hire you
or if you would ever be one of those "successful" people.

When you end up broke and alone
after years of doing alright,
don't forget how you once longed for
the challenge and freedom of starting from zero.

When you get caught up in the little dramas
and ups and downs of city life,
don't forget the perfect calm of stepping outside
and feeling the breeze on your face as
you gazed into the abyss of sky.

When you lose sight of why you love life
and don't see the point of going on,
don't forget how infinite and tiny you felt
fording these streams and hiking past the horizon.

Don't forget this time when you were exposed
fully and humbly to the elements and the unknown.

Don't forget this feeling
that you are unsure and afraid
and vulnerable and free,
and that whether or not you end up where you'd planned,
life will go on.

Welcome P.C.T. Hikers

Crater Lake National Park really does **not** want you here.

- **NO** camping within 1 mile of road.
- **NO** camping between the road and the rim.
- **NO** hitchhiking within the park.

* We spend your tax dollars enforcing these rules and building more roads through the park, rather than maintaining trails.

*** Please come back when you have a car and money to spend in the gift shop.

This is a sacred place, but they don't seem to see. They zoom by in their cars and purchase their souvenirs and take their photos. They speed over the pumice field on their motorbikes and toss wrappers out of their RV windows. Chained to their need for comfort they fail to see what is here. They do not hear the birds chattering or see the marmots playing or feel the soft lake breeze on their bare skin. Despite all of the obvious signs that this ancient place was not made solely for their enjoyment, they come here with their blind sense of entitlement and seem to leave with nothing more or less. They do not want to hear about the endangered White Bark Pine or about the people who were here before our roads intruded. They want to drive by the scenic overlooks and eat their soft-serve ice cream without guilt and drive back to their safe hotel beds to worship the moving pictures trapped in a plastic box. But this place is old and rugged and real, and it will remain long after they have gone.

BACK TO NORTHBOUND!

Mile 2138
INDIAN SPRING
(Abandoned) CAMPGROUND

RAMONA FALLS

Day 116
August 17th

SANDY RIVER CROSSING   Mile 2117

Indian Spring C.G. Mile 2138

August 18th

Day 117

EAGLE CREEK

Cascade Locks! Mile 2155

Best Western

Mom, Nini, Bill — Parents on a Buffalo

Portland!

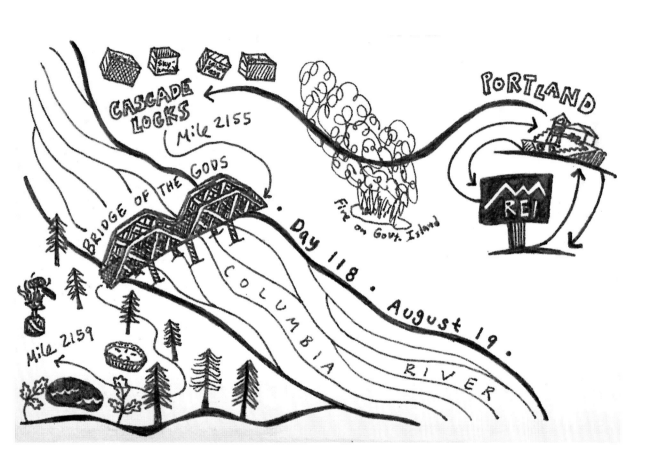

Things Thru-Hikers Have in Common with 5-Year-Olds, A Surprisingly Extensive List:

- Eating Pop-Tarts and candy bars all day
- Needing an afternoon nap
- Getting really excited about McDonald's or root beer floats
- Depending on other people for car rides
- Smelling bad
- Being covered in dirt
- Being unemployed... ... ...

- Wearing the same clothes every day
- Not seeing anything wrong with accepting candy from strangers
- Going by silly nicknames
- Drinking soda whenever given the opportunity
- Going to bed by 8'oclock
- Sleepovers!
- Becoming BEST FRIENDS with people you just met... ...

- Talking about poop and farts
- Shamelessly picking your nose and farting in public
- Realizing that you need to poop RIGHT NOW
- Eating food off of the ground
- Carrying a backpack
- Constantly comparing the coolness of your stuff to everyone else's
- Getting jealous of other people's lunches
- Having emotional meltdowns on a fairly regular basis
- Asking everyone else what they're doing before making your own decisions
- Having parents who worry if you don't check in often enough...

- Being repeatedly told about the dangers of playing with fire
- Getting grumpy if you don't get your snack or nap
- Going straight for the candy aisle in the grocery store
- Always wanting more dessert
- Poking things with sticks
- Walking places in lines
- Talking to yourself and creating elaborate fantasy worlds in your head
- Being blissfully ignorant of current events
- Feeling small compared to everything around you
- Playing outside

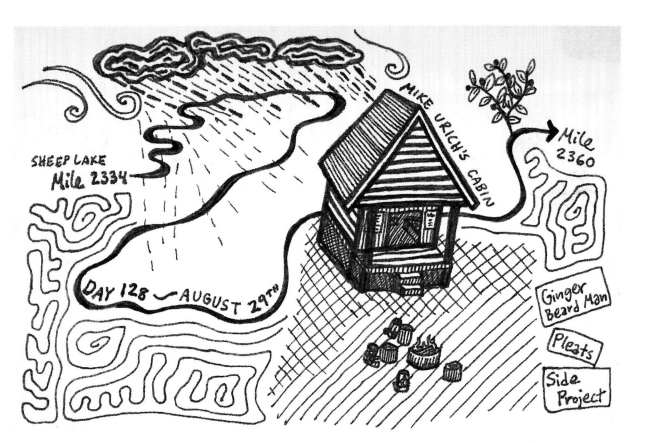

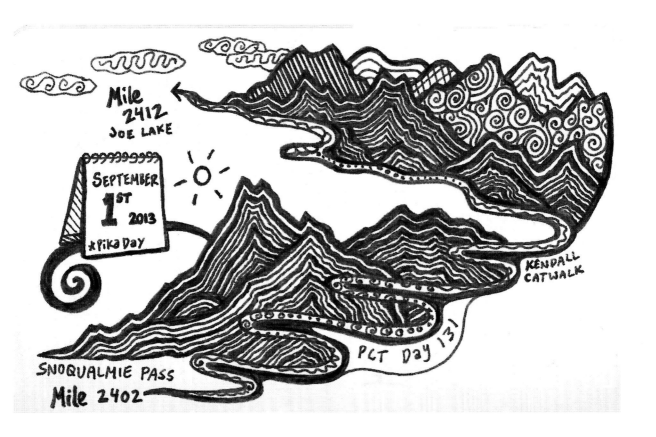

September 6th
Day 136

Mile 2478

Mile 2494

Tea Bag
Scabby
Chief
Slack
Red Beard
Thunder Song
Kindergarten Cop

PEAR LAKE

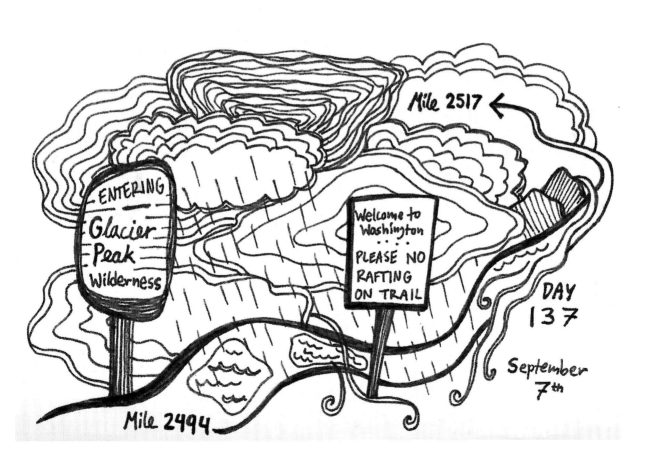

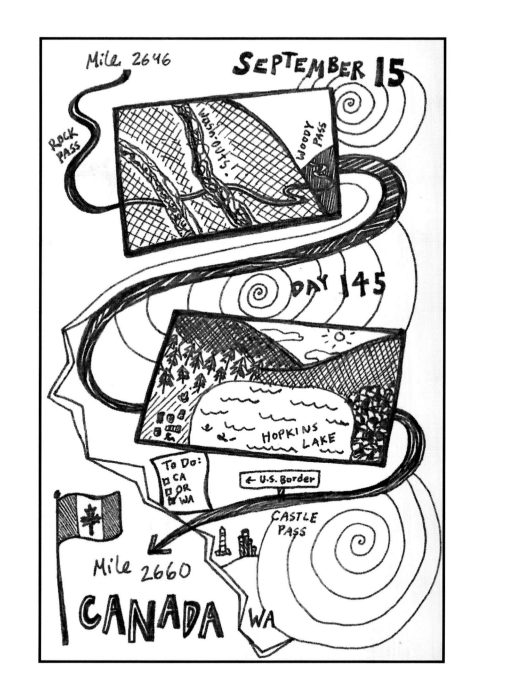

CAKE! SOUP! FOCACCIA BREAD!

Quinoa Lasagna

GREEN BEANS!

MANNING PARK

Parents on a Buffalo! | Kilian | Matthew | Tony

MILE 2668

Oh Canada! My home and native land — True patriots' love, in all thy sons' command — with glowing hearts, we see the rise, the true North strong and free — From far and wide, O-oh Canada, we stand on guard for thee — God keep our land,

SEPTEMBER 16 • PCT DAY 146 • MILE 2660

glorious and free — Oh Canada we stand on guard for theeee — Oh Canada we stand on guard for thee!

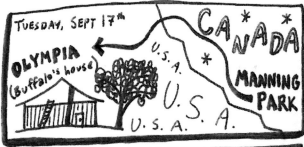

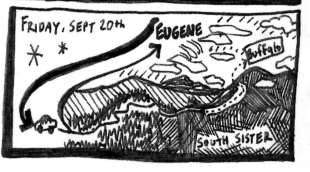

From Manning Park, we took the better part of a week to make our way back down to Crater Lake to begin the 320-mile section that the smoke had pushed us to skip earlier in the trip. Our second arrival to Crater Lake was greeted by temperatures in the low thirties and a windy mixture of something between rain and snow. Feeling more than ready to be home, I opted to end my hike there and return to Portland that day, while Claire and Buffalo decided to tough out the weather and push on to the end. I spent a lovely two weeks at home drinking lots of tea, and they both completed their thru-hike in Castella, CA in mid-October.

Thank You...

To all of the wonderful trail angels who helped us out along the way: Dr. Sole, Mike Herrera, Kennedy Meadows Tom, Kushy, Ziggy and the Bear, Mike and Patricia, Donna Saufley, Papa Smurf, Yogi and Okie Girl and Jackelope and Bear Bait, Gantt, ALOHA, Trapper-Keeper, Hellen and Chuck & Colleen and Robin.

To the PCTA, Halfmile, and Craig (of Craig's PCT Planner).

To all of the people responsible for making the following places along the trail so welcoming: Warner Springs, Hiker Heaven, Tehachapi, Kennedy Meadows, VVR, Sierra City, Old Station, Big Lake Youth Camp, Timberline Lodge, Stehekin.

To everyone who set up and maintained water caches along the trail. To everyone who left out coolers of drinks or snacks for passing hikers. To everyone who gave us a ride into town or back to the trail.

To everyone who followed our blog and supported and encouraged us from back home.

To all of the friends and family who came out to see us on the trail, brought us food, hosted us, and/or gave us rides: Namo, Super-Ultra-Light, Buffalo's Parents, Colin and Cathy, All of the Family at Black Butte, Joan and Dave and Carmen and Remy, Everyone who joined us for Claire's Birthday at Timberline, Patti, my brother Alex, Nini and Bill, Dave and Beth, Lilly, Susan and Richard and Bella and Dylan.

...Thank You...

To all of the other 2013 hikers who made the trail community so much fun, especially: Rum Monkey, Hummingbird, Mudd and Dingo, Lotus and Hermes, Noah the Prophet, Yusuke, Golden Hour and NoDay, Shotput, Pepper Flake, Maggie, Jess, Mr. Green, PRT, Sunshine, Dog, Boulder and Scoots, Sour Cream, LunchBox, Dance Party, T-Rex (who also took the photo below), The WolfPack, Turtle and Silver, Happy Hour and Squeaks, Shedder and Roo, Frosty and G-Locks, Siesta, Long Legs and Jorge, Pel-Mel and La-Ti-Da.

To Guy on a Buffalo for hiking over 1000 miles with us, carrying whole pies on top of your pack, being a badass, and sticking with us through everything.

To Ann Marie Lei for all of your love and logistical support.

To Skip Lei for suggesting that I do a "doodle a day" during this trip.

To everyone who looked at my doodle journal along the way and said something along the lines of: "Have you thought about publishing this..."

About the Artist

Katie Lei was born in 1989 in Portland, Oregon. She studied French Literature at Whitman College, where she doodled in the margins of her notebooks and cultivated her love of the outdoors by working part-time as a rock climbing instructor and Outdoor Program trip leader. She graduated in 2012 and decided to put her liberal arts degree to good use by embarking on a year of adventures, including the Pacific Crest Trail.